THESE DAYS

THESE DAYS

Leontia Flynn

CAPE POETRY

Published by Jonathan Cape 2004

4 6 8 10 9 7 5

First published in Great Britain in 2004 by
Jonathan Cape
Random House, 20 Vauxhall Bridge Road, London SW1V 2SA

Random House Australia (Pty) Limited
20 Alfred Street, Milsons Point, Sydney,
New South Wales 2061, Australia

Random House New Zealand Limited
18 Poland Road, Glenfield,
Auckland 10, New Zealand

Random House South Africa (Pty) Limited
Endulini, 5a Jubilee Road, Parktown, 2193, South Africa

The Random House Group Limited Reg. No. 954009
www.randomhouse.co.uk

A CIP catalogue record for this book
is available from the British Library

ISBN 0-224-07197-1

Papers used by Random House are natural,
recyclable products made from wood grown in sustainable forests,
the manufacturing processes conform to the environmental
regulations of the country of origin.

Typeset by Palimpsest Book Production Limited, Polmont, Stirlingshire
Printed and bound in Great Britain by Biddles Ltd, King's Lynn, Norfolk

For Karen O'Reilly

CONTENTS

ACKNOWLEDGEMENTS

Some of these poems have originally appeared in *Envoi, Fortnight, The Irish University Review, London Magazine, New Soundings* (Blackstaff), *Poetry Ireland Review, Product, Proof, The Shop* and *Staying Alive* (Bloodaxe).

Acknowledgements are due to The Arts Council of Northern Ireland for a bursary in 2000 – which allowed me to purchase my computer – as well as, very particularly, to Belfast City Council for funding a residency at Annaghmakkerig in 2001, and to the British Council in Belfast for sending me to Budapest in 2003. I also have to thank my friends and family – and Lawrence Warnett for writing the code for 'Perl Poem'.

NAMING IT

Five years out of school and preachy
with booklearning, it is good to be discovered
as a marauding child.
To think the gloomiest most baffled
misadventures might lead so suddenly
to a clearing – as when a friend
taking me to her well-stocked fridge says:
look
this is an avocado and *this*
is an aubergine.

ACTS OF FAITH

On my 24th birthday
my lungs close over, tight as a baby's fist
round its first rattle.
It might be the Holy Ghost,
the disc of light skittering on the ceiling
thrown up from the paten on a water-glass
which my mother brings with Prednisone.
She sings Happy Birthday Happy Birthday
and tells me, as she has always done,
that she would take my place. I believe her.

EEPS

So I'm wondering was my father a prophet
when – as often – one of his little wires came loose
in the light fitting with the brass surround on our white
    porch wall

and he hauled us – we were seven – in crocodile
    formation
to the scrubbed white porch with the faulty light fitting,
where he planted his thumb – like a crocodile-clip – to
    the brass

– and the base, like a touch-paper, crackled – as wild
    eeps and ozone
went flocking – not minding the gap – to the end of the
    line
which might now be this scattered, flickering parish

the quick jab on the X key; this brief thrill on the
    hand . . .

COME LIVE WITH ME

Come live with me and be my mate
and all the fittings and the fixtures of the flat
will bust with joy –

                    this flowered ottoman, this tallboy.
I'll leave a water-ring around your heart.
In the mildewed kitchenette of afternoon
T.V., my cup of coffee
overfloweth. *Neighbours. Ironside.*
Whatever Happened to Baby Jane?
– that well-known scene in which, as you explain, the
    feral heel
Of Bette Davis meets Ms Crawford's head – head on –
    for real! for real!

WITHOUT ME

Without me you have gone astray, I know
I have launched you into the three-dimensional
    afternoon
like that image of the mother on the first school
    morning
prodding her eldest child towards the door.
And the days spent steadily stuffing my head with this,
your days spent walking in the public sector –
the parks, the museums and the libraries
with the mad old fuckers muttering into the
    microfiche –
these days run back to the dark pool of our nights
and the silent levelling of water.

FOR STUART,
WHO ACCIDENTALLY OBTAINED
A JOB IN THE CIVIL SERVICE

I have it in my diary as May the 6th
and a beautiful evening. We walk in silence
back to my house. There are condolences;
sitting round as though we are at a wake,
somebody mentions Kafka.

You explain about your mother.
For now, I tell you, just for now . . .
the evening light and a spark, fallen
from your cigarette butt onto the woolly jumper
over your truculent heart, quietly dying.

DONEGAL

When the snooze function on your alarm clock goes a
    third time
and light, straining at the window, has thinned to a
    skimmed milk,
there would be as much point in us calling out to you
as there would be in us calling to Mont Blanc.

There would be as much point trying to stir you as
    your cold coffee.
This waste of crusted cups, this waste of crusted plates,
the bony hills of your old duvet
the lamp, giving its spud-coloured 40 watts,

is your reserve: your dark little landscape
rolled over again, unconscious, on its hip.

FESTIVAL TIME

Three weeks after midsummer night
a shudder runs up the spine of the terraces
and along the pulse. If my mother phones
tell her I'm not in. She's pleading:
Get out. Get out of there now. Come home.

But I don't know anything about anything
and it feels almost like a festival time – to turn the key,
to collapse in bed at dawn punchdrunk, fiddling
with the radio dial, with each other
While Rome Burns.

GAMES

They have taken Kevin off the machine for Christmas.
The lights are on –
but his mouth keeps working, over and over:
Ouzo. Sambuca. Jägermeister.
We hold his free hand like the string of a kite.

Later that night, it's a double shot in the dark:
retracing our steps from A to A
and the flat where we learned, strategically, to down a
   bridge
        too far –
We move beyond the pint of no return.

BRINKWOMANSHIP

When they come for you no bigger than a piece of fruit,
weighing no more and no less than a water biscuit,
this will be my excuse:
that I hoped you were just testing yourself
as I might subtly and irresistibly
poke at a sensitive tooth. That is, not morbidly,
but out of a curiosity
to locate the exact, minute, sensory transition – between
merely knowing the definition
of pain, and knowing the *meaning*.

HERE

As if this would sum it up:
the slow elision of the days they tell you
will begin in autumn when everything
is over. Emptyhanded. The white grain
of each afternoon in succession – like crossing a road
with the sun in your eyes, stepping in front of a car
driven by an old friend, her head
poking out of the window. You check your pulse.
She asks:
Are you still *here*?

THE AMAZING, DISAPPEARING

A morning routine, anaesthetic
as passing your finger through a candle
if you can just do it quickly enough.
Socks.
      Shoes.
           A hasty exit.
'Mister' to the mail arriving misdirected
and mis-spelt; 'Hey!' to the winos
cooling their heels by the shopfronts and trafficlights;
and even a 'Lady'
to the parent warning her headlong, crashing child:
'Watch out for that –'

THE SECOND MRS DE WINTER

Last night they dreamt of her again,
my falafel-cooking predecessor.
Of how she would have the flat hysterical,
when in her opulent cups, with the one about the
    three men,
the three men, I think, and the greyhound.

I am the second Mrs de Winter:
cack-handed, fumbling a jar
of sushi in ginger, cracking the noseable bowl
of a fine, long-stemmed wineglass
while my original stares, implacable, from the wall.

WITHOUT ME

Without me, you have been exactly that.
I have launched you nowhere. I have launched myself
no further than this desk and west-facing window
where were I to keep a calm and vigilant reach
I would hold the weeks and months from filling a breach
that makes unbridgeable your rooms at Rushfield,
the days when you took the clockwork out of things
striking a new sound from a dud motor.
When we meet now, we cannot but be slightly older.
Outside. Under a ticking, bewildered sky.

WITHOUT ME

Without me and without you, what's the point
of the fact that you fried onions like you were
   harpooning shrimp
in a wok found in a skip near a flat on Wellesley?
And what's the point of the three-and-a-half years spent
– like fifteen minutes at a bus-stop – if as casually
as my glib wave, when something moves from my hand,
or the road receding in the driver's mirror,
we are gone?
               Suddenly it's beyond me:
how I'm turning my thoughts to the bird or two in the
   bush
and to all the fish in the intervening sea.

Walking with him was like walking somehow in shadow.
The sun went out of her way to keep us in the dark.
Once, I was told, as he was entering a friend's house
the lightbulbs – even the fridge's – exploded in
    splintering hail.
And it should have been easy had he not broken every
    rule
like when I awoke – I had laboured, his little
    handmaiden! –
to find him by the bedside: his face, in a kind of cloud,
was the face of a stranger; and so I dozed again,
and so I woke – to find him, in negative, lying
– like the Turin Shroud – on this white sheet of my
    memory.

WITHOUT ME

Without me I have been without you I
have lost my bearings I have lost the key
on the heart-shaped fob – the talisman you gave me.

July the tenth, 1999
and from the sky comes the Great King of Terror.

But Sylvia gulps a paroxetine with soda
and snaps – with her teeth – the magic thread
whose breadth is a hair-trigger.

So, Sylvia, go on, snap the magic thread
between feeling – feeling everything, feeling nothing.

ON THE THIRD FLOOR OF THE
ROYAL INFIRMARY

On the third floor of the Royal Infirmary
She makes a dash from the lift – And Is Gone.
Scattering birds from the bells,
She would set tongues wagging around the city.
Weeping, she fingers her Yamaha during the small hours.

Because something has made a nonsense of her.
Now she can no more look, cold-eyed, in a looking glass
than I at this. The doctors told her:
Congratulations Miss, your face
has given birth
                        to a new face.

WHEN I WAS SIXTEEN I MET
SEAMUS HEANEY

When I was sixteen I met Seamus Heaney
outside a gallery in Dublin. I was with a friend
who knew her way around better than I did.
She was carrying Flann O'Brien's *The Poor Mouth*.

As I have it Heaney winked when he signed her copy
of *The Poor Mouth*. He said: That's a great book.
I ground my teeth: she hadn't even *read* it.
It was summer: UV-haze, bitumen fumes, etc.

I had read *The Poor Mouth* – but who was Seamus
    Heaney?
I believe he signed my bus ticket, which I later lost.

MY DREAM MENTOR

My dream mentor sits in his room overlooking the city.
He can see the far swell of the Pentlands, the folk milling
    below
hapless as maggots. So we sit there in silence
like a couple of kids in the bath, till he says:

If you can't be a prodigy, there's no point trying.
Don't fall for the one about the drunk, queuing in
    Woolworths,
who tells you his Gaelic opus was seized by the state.
If you can fashion something with a file in it for the
    academics
to hone their malicious nails on – you're minted.
And another thing, don't write about anything
                                    you can point at.

SNOW

When the academic year of a millennium
winds itself, wheezily, into the siding
where will you find me?

Running like a girl
for the love of a fast-track train
back to the fish-smelling ferry terminal.
The sea raises a glass – rosé – to the sky at Troon.

But something is blocking the line.
It's leaves perhaps – or that other obstinate cliché:
the wrong kind of snow.

NOCTURNE

Trying to figure that *je ne sais quoi* a poem takes to get
    published:
a clerical temp, capitalising on the caesura
in his working day – sweet little night enjambing
from the blue scraps of his evening.

He is sat with a pointed stick by this sheet of fly-paper,
the words not coming.
(Though his lines are coming down with feminine
    endings.)

My tongue cleaves to my mouth O Lord, The Words
    not coming
he writes, The Words not . . . Wha?
      Whaddya mean already written? What?
Louis? Louis who?

WITHOUT ME

Once, in the hiatus of a difficult July,
down Eskra's lorryless roads from sweet fuck all,
we were flinging – such young sophisticates – like a giant
    frisbee
this plastic lid of an old rat-poison bin.

We were flinging it from you to me, me to you, you to
    me;
me-you, you-me, me-you, you back again.
And you would have sworn that its flat arc was a
    pendulum,
compassing Tyrone's prosy horizon.

And I would have sworn that our throw and catch had
    such momentum
that its rhythm might survive, somehow, without me.

WHAT YOU GET

Two roads diverge in South Gyle Industrial Estate
and you would take the one less travelled by
if it were not, you think, possibly the cul-de-sac
where the snack vans park at night, or where the trucks
are moored, fed and watered, after their delivery
of precious things.
                    One afternoon you watch
as a host of Styrofoam balls comes billowing through
and covers the close: a great Andrei Tarkovsky
slo-mo, and you're pleased with it –
its basic wage, take-what-you-get epiphany.

TWO CROSSINGS

In a boat full of people travelling from Stranraer,
the air gathered under the marquee of the cabin seems to
    be alive
with one leviathan and clattering *accent*.
This is the kind of boat that pretends not to be.
It could be snowing over the sea right now but we are
    sealed in, airless,
the students mostly lashed to the bar,
and other folk gloomily and gradually congregating in
    the diner
which sells chickenbones in batter in a basket.

One of my miserable neighbours is a gigantic beery man
with a moustache. He is complaining loudly
because one of his party didn't receive their free drink.
He tells them: if you don't complain about nuthin,
nuthin is ever done. The wind starts picking up.
I remember one rough crossing when a woman in a
    wheelchair
was carried back and forth by the boat's rocking
for the length of a corridor between two glass doors.

I must have watched her, helpless, for one minute, two
    minutes . . .
And now the wind is taking hold of this boat
as surely as the half-walnut shell with the tiny sail.
People quit moonwalking the deck and collapse into
    seats.
A waitress dives over to clear up and to ask was every-
    thing alright?

The miserables tell her it was, thankyou,
thankyou very much – and we are half asleep with this
   rocking
as the boat approaches the harbour and home.

DOYNE

Everyone planned it to remember just where they'd been
and what they'd been doing. Kiribati, Auckland, Sydney,
Port Moresby, Tokyo. At the last of the bells

I let my tongue from your cheek for just long enough
to have you practising your Doyne, Soyth Doyne, Soyth –
till my eyes rolled up, two zeros in 2000.

PET DEATHS

for Harvey

We were in two camps over the man in Edinburgh
who threw his dog off North Bridge,
then jumped himself.
                              Some said
it was kind of a *suttee*: a failure of imagination,
'That dog was not the man's left arm', they said.
Others pointed out that the dog might have pined
or starved anyway.

My first death was a dog. There were no
minor heresies on my parents' part. No
loving blasphemies to fool the kids
that this lassie-come-home of my childhood,
                                        who herded us
close to the ditch down country lanes, and who
– dying of meningitis no less – still sprinted the mile
   back
to where my father stood whistling,
                                        had gone to heaven.

Now we have our own pet deaths:
this is pluralism. And channel-surfing
between half-hearted atheism, superstitious Zen,
                                        I still see Harvey
– our late lamented dog; the terrier of my adolescence –
his cataracts clear, his bite returned and his tail wagging
one day spinning with me forever
from some bridge of oblivion.

A PAUSE

There is a pause in the middle of conversation
during which time we absently get to our feet
put on our coats, our terrible secondhand hats,
and walk for fifteen minutes to the demolished all-night
  shop.

When we return, what stops us isn't the locks
– which won't have changed, like the ancient décor:
(the 'chesterfield suite', the oiled patch, like an
  antimacassar
where you rested your head, that flock

wallpaper) – but the sight of our small brick
garden, thick with dandelion clocks.

IT'S A WONDERFUL LIFE

Somewhere between five and seven in the morning
to gauge by the light and inferior type of talk show
we have hatched an inspired plan – we are weak, frazzled
    and salivating –
our masterstroke, the apotheosis of our lives.

They will find us bobbing – like frozen corks – under
    the eaves
Of some bridge or other – the Albert? The Ormeau?
'A Tragic and Apocalyptic Act.' The lights will fade
– the water will be cool and clear terrible as celluloid –

as the score crescendos. No one, in the end,
will make jokes about fish – of any size – or about small
    ponds.

BRIDGES

For 64,000 what's Paris's oldest bridge?
The Pont Neuf? The Pont Royale? We can't remember
  which is which.
And the days are too long, and the nights are too long,
And life lounges late on the sofa – Not. Flipping. That.
  Switch.

BED POEM

bed, the word, is almost a child's
picture poem, a hieroglyph spelling itself:
the stroke of the b forming a bedpost on one side
and the stroke of the d the bedpost on the other.

Surely, at some stage – perhaps
down the black pits of winter mornings – everyone
has felt the urge to go Florence Nightingale:

                                               just

forget this whole business of penetrating
and directing a day. Take to our lazy beds.
Let the days have their way with us.

Imagine the heavy comfort of curtains . . .
I would lay my ear to the mattress and test the weight
   of bed words:

  moony   goosefeather   incubus

against my tongue. I would listen to the deep
grinding harmonies of the bedsprings.

PERL POEM

Surrounded by bric-a-brac – mugs of stale coffee and old
    manuals – Lawrence works at his desk.
His computer screen burns like a Cyclops' eye. He is
    writing programs
for drinks companies in Dublin – helping keep Ireland,
    North and South, awash with hooch.

```
while( <FHND> ){ s/\x0a/\x0d\x0a/g; push(
   @m_arr, Hio:parse( $_ ) ); }..., he writes,
for ( $i; $i < @m_arr; $i++ ) { print FHND
   $m_arr[ $i ]; }.
```

Programming language, he says, is no dry, fussy
    abstraction. There's tremendous wit
in its usage: the elegance of Perl – Edwin Morgin's 'great,
    final ease of creation'
in tuning the lines most perfectly to their function. It's
    not science fiction.
It's not like: *If we can just hack into the mainframe of the*
    computer
we should be able to upload the virus on to the mothership.

And it's not like poetry; it doesn't log out or go off into
    the ether freighted only with itself;
it walks a network of roads, getting dust on its feet and
    saying hi to people –

```
sub cZap { my $sig = shift; &cleanup; die
   "Recd: SIG$sig\n"; } $SIG{ INT} = \&cZap; -
```

It doesn't hover over the country – like poetry does –
    like a special effect.

GRANITE

One Saturday in preparation for the trip
you show me on the Phillips atlas –
yellowish, wrinkled like cellulite, between granite
and the deep blue sea loch –
where your father dredged a channel
through the landscape of your childhood,
with a pipe and a periscope.

Don't worry he told you. With the blast-centre
this close, it's bang, lights out:
there'd be nothing left but the ringing granite.
Your boyhood a magnesium puff
and no time for that sickening wind
to mosey at leisure through the burns and bracken
or arrive downwind at the shipshape house

where later you sealed your bedroom door
with a pile of sodden clothes
you had worn for days; washed the door handle
seven times (taking care that the washcloth
touched neither the heel of your hand, nor the wrist) –
and then counted the pills
into piles of seven. You were sixteen.

THE FRANKLIN'S TALE

Reading The Franklin's Tale. It is 1993
and I am 18. Dorigen
cries for her love out over the water:

Lord, thise grisley fiendly rokkes blake.
In class we call it nonsense. Gibberish.
It is 1993. And we are reading Chaucer

of all things. We drink instant coffee.
We discuss Miro and Hieronymus Bosch.
We say: 'I am not going to be a teacher'

and mean it. Because we mean everything.
Near my exams I do something extraordinary.
I begin driving round in a white Toyota Corolla.

We park by the low wall of the harbour.
The lights from the town. I say 'Heathcliff!'
and we are more wrapped up in each other

than a *creel of eels*. Than glue.
Than the Guggenheim.
From this, my most complicated summer

I let myself out, like thread from a spool, slowly,
sometimes – even The Franklin's Tale –
calling back to it, like love, across the water.

APRIL, 7 P.M.

Where our phone wires meet
over those terraces – look
the sky is still blue!

THE MYTH OF TEA BOY

Every evening, at the same time, Tea Boy comes into the
    shop
and orders his regular, please. If he thinks he is getting
    Earl Grey
and the brew in our teapot is sometimes, more or less,
    Tetley,
then nobody acts the wiser; the fronts on the Golden
    Mile,
their windows rinsed by the sun, go on cranking out
    their awnings
and espresso machines – and we'll act like we're in diners
from everyone's favourite Hopper poster, Nighthawks.

All of the waitresses, and even some of the waiters,
    secretly believe
it is to see her, or to see him, in particular, that every
    evening
Tea Boy pays this call. His cup rests on the intersection
of four or five sideways glances from our busy spots
    round the floor.
As the room fills up with 'Eternal Flame': the cover
    version, on the radio,
and, floor to ceiling, the last of the summer light, we also
    know
for as long as this pose is held we won't spill a single
    drop.

THE MORNING AFTER RUTH'S
GOING-AWAY PARTY

The morning after Ruth's going-away party
the state of this place is its testament, like Pompeii.
The needle snags on the record and then snags again
and Karen Carpenter sings we've only, we've only just
   begun.

HOLLAND

I

The rattling noise from the heater in the daffodil shed
has assumed the rhythm of the production line
where now you continually pack and unpack yourself;
it's insane that in the longest part of the night
there's a moment to think of Larkin's 'incessant recital'
in *If, my Darling* – was *this* what he meant?
This world unpicked by 'meaning and meaning's
    rebuttal'?

II

The Dutch doctor with the brunette handlebar
    moustache
smiles sadly as he prescribes Oxazypam
(are these *cow* tranquillisers?), giving a little shrug
at his own proposal to 'avoid these with alcohol',
then taking your grime-stained urchin's hand, he adds
'If I live in Belfast, I also perhaps feel bad'.
Now even your *neuroses* are unoriginal.

THE MAGICIAN

Since you first developed an understanding of gravity
things no longer dropped so much as were 'let fall';
the floor of your room – like a stretch of desert plain –
is littered as though with wagon hoops and cattle skulls.

With your surf sandals, marigold gloves and unfastened
    hair
You wander round the kitchen looking like Aphrodite;
you turn receipts to mâché, oxidise keys, begin to launder
    money,
even washing water – just, you say, 'to be sure'.

If a door slams, dust rises, or something in particular is
    moved
your hands might suddenly become as furred and fugged
as if you had touched the fur of a terrible dog.

And when you stretch your arm into the drum of the
    Creda
I think you might extract, as though from my sleeve,
A row of brightly coloured silk handkerchiefs.

SATIS HOUSE

Late summer light is slanting through the glass:
a frieze of light on the carpet, an indiscreet freeze-frame
of all the junk and clutter of this place –
something is playing out, and we have set the scene:
a column of smoke rising up from an ashtray
then stuttering out; the sunlight's indiscreet snapshot
of slumped clothes and old newsprint, of ring-pulls and
    bottle caps,
loose change, the last of your Lustral – spilled salt.

★

'Who *lives* in a house like this?' I quote
with my usual gift for avoiding 'the issues' with humour
when I find you standing, intent, by the kitchen counter
grouping the bottles like a family photograph;
or when I scuba through the hallway's submarine gloom
into the empty bathroom's particular squalor,
and, lifting a plug of hair from the plughole of the bath,
find that it's followed by your vigilant head and
    shoulders.

★

Bored with our décor and colour scheme, we revamp
our living space with little tricks, encourage the wiring,
already erratic, to scorch the walls; we bloat the doors
    with damp,
perfume the rooms with mildew – and something more
    troubling.
Entertaining? We've laid on this great and mouldering
    spread;

if the doorbell rings, both of us bolt for cover,
me stepping, in turn, through the rooms of your dirty
    mind,
blowing, with my usual verve, one bulb after the other.

*

Late summer light is slanting through the glass
on our knee-deep junk and clutter, on all the decisions
yet to be made – a kind of history of our shiftlessness.
Outside 'small towns heap up on the horizon',
and big things hang in the balance. Here in silence
darkness and dust are gathering round this place
– then falling, taking the path of least resistance.

BOYS

When Philomena Guinea telegrams 'Is there a boy in the
    case?'
having read about Esther Greenwood in a Boston paper
– Esther Greenwood being, at this point, incarcerated –
you shut, abruptly, your copy of *The Bell Jar*
and deposit the book on the desk of your teenager's
    room
with *A Passage to India* (its Boom Ou Boom Ou Boom):
if there *is*, Mrs Guinea can have nothing 'of course' to do
    with it.

If there's a boy in the case Mrs Guinea cannot be
    involved
and your mother would like to know if you're wise or
    what
– when the world should be your oyster for heaven's
    sake –
to be moping about all hours of the day and night;
and to be singing along with the records you play on
    repeat,
that only love can break
your heart yes only love can break your heart.

THE MAN WITH THE HATCHET

Drive me home again
so that the street lights loom
and orbit the car like moons
which set in the back seat.

Because now in the darkness
that legendary man in the back with the hatchet
will show his eyes over my shoulder
in the rear-view mirror.

FOR LILY ALLEN

At ten o'clock as Heather's labour starts
the traffic is a stream of cells, a path of dithering
    corpuscles,
though the call comes through that puts us on Red Alert;
she has asked along one person for competence, a standby
    for good luck,
and me, she says, in order to 'make her laugh'.

But the traffic dithers between us, and I'm suddenly miles
    away,
mentally shuffling my script, filching a pen from the
    nurse
– something, inexorably, forms on the tip of my tongue –
then I lose the thread – with her pain and pain relief
    and by afternoon
unanswerably, she's delivered the kid like a punchline.

IT'S A WONDERFUL LIFE

I had been dragging my feet, as though across the sea
    bed,
watching the same birds wheel over the old market
    places,
when, walking through town – the way a dame walks in
    with a gun
and a flagging crime plot revives – suddenly, from-
    nowhere, the sun
had thrown her weight behind the afternoon's open
    spaces.

I had been turning towards the quays when this, the eye
    of the storm,
passed over without a fuss: there was no fight, no flight,
and the sea – which had been so restless – for now was
    written in stone.
Leaving the air flocking and beating around the still
    wings of gulls,
leaving the flagstones at my feet, which were beginning
    to lap and ripple.

THE FURTHEST DISTANCES I'VE TRAVELLED

Like many folk, when first I saddled a rucksack,
feeling its weight on my back –
the way my spine
curved under it like a meridian –

I thought: Yes. This is how
to live. On the beaten track, the sherpa pass, between
    Krakow
and Zagreb, or the Siberian white
cells of scattered airports,

it came clear as over a tannoy
that in restlessness, in anony
mity:
was some kind of destiny.

So whether it was the scare stories about Larium
– the threats of delirium
and baldness – that led me, not to a Western Union
wiring money with six words of Lithuanian,

but to this post office with a handful of bills
or a giro; and why, if I'm stuffing smalls
hastily into a holdall, I am less likely
to be catching a Greyhound from Madison to
    Milwaukee

than to be doing some overdue laundry
is really beyond me.
However,
when, during routine evictions, I discover

alien pants, cinema stubs, the throwaway
comment – on a Post-it – or a tiny stowaway
pressed flower amid bottom drawers,
I know these are my souvenirs

and, from these crushed valentines, this unravelled
sports sock, that the furthest distances I've travelled
have been those between people. And what survives
of holidaying briefly in their lives.

Last night I dreamt that I was 26,
the age my mother was when she married
and shunted from her crowded homestead in the city
into a solitary bungalow built by my father;
looking over the stubbly field she gave up
this last unholy qualm: what have I done?

My father still lived in a village in County Down
at – for him – the adolescent age of 26.
There was a long tot machine which could add up
and subtract accounts (my grandmother had married
a tradesman) at the yank of a stiff lever:
a gadget charming, he says, in its simplicity.

My parents met at a dancehall in the city.
I see her in a sleeveless dress, perhaps, sitting down
and my jug-eared and inimitable father
considering that he is no longer 26 –
he's beginning to feel the minuses of the unmarried.
He smokes the fags that later she makes him give up

and crosses the dance floor. Would my mother get up
and dance with him? Outside the city
is in darkness: industrial but unhurried.
A slight, predictable rain is falling down.
My mother, who is not yet 26,
agrees to dance one dance with my jug-eared father.

This is the turning point. This is the father
of all love stories: the moment they give up
the multiple things of life round 26.
The lights in the dancehall shift in intensity;
the mirror ball throws snowflakes in a meltdown.
26, they say, is a good age to get married

or to do something momentous like get married.
These are the past lives of my mother and father
which have come to me in fragments, handed down
like a solvable puzzle – ready to give up
some clue to the possibilities of the city
that my mother left when she was 26.

Last night I dreamt that I was 26 and married
to the city. Under a fog, the voice of my father:
What will you give up? What will be handed down?

BY MY SKIN

for Terry McGaughey

Mr Bennet in *Pride and Prejudice – The Musical!*,
my father communicates with his family almost entirely
    through song.
From the orange linoleum and trumpet-sized wallpaper
    flowers
of the late 1970s, he steps with a roll of cotton,
a soft-shoe routine, and a pound of soft white paraffin.

He sings 'Oft in the Stilly Night' and 'Believe Me, If All
    Those Endearing Young Charms'.
He sings 'Edelweiss' and 'Cheek to Cheek' from *Top Hat*.
Disney-animals are swaying along the formica sink-top
where he gets me into a lather. He greases behind my
    knees
and the folds of my elbows; he wraps me in swaddling
    clothes.

Then lifts me up with his famous high-shouldered shuffle
– 'Yes Sir, That's My Baby!' – to the candlewick bunk.
The air is bright with a billion exfoliate flitters
as he changes track – one for his changeling child:
Hauld Up Your head My Bonnie Wee Lass and Dinnae
    Look So Shy.

He sings 'Put Your Shoes On, Lucy (Don't You Know
    You're In The City)'.
He sings 'Boolavogue' and 'Can't Help Loving that Man
    of Mine'
and 'Lily the Pink' and 'The Woods of Gortnamona'.
He sings – the lights are fading – Slievenamon
And about the 'Boy Blue' (who awakens 'to angel song')

My father is Captain Von Trapp, Jean Valjean, Professor
    Henry Higgins –
gathering his repertoire, with the wheatgerm and
    cortisone,
like he's gathering up a dozen tribute roses.
Then, taking a bow, he lays these – just so – by my skin
which gets better and worse, and worse and better again.

MANGLES

Washboards and mangles are on my father's mind.
In conversation he will return to the soaked linen
of his childhood – its labour-intensiveness –
as though these shirts and sheets, ready for the line,
floated behind my head in a basin together

and he could reach across and bring them in
amazed how they come up white again and again
after all these years – the marriage, the
   'money-grubbing',
the household overrun by lunatic women
putting one thing after another through the wringer.

THESE DAYS

for Catherine Donnelly

These days, it seems, I am winding my clock an hour
    forward
with every second weekend, and the leaves on my Marc
    Chagall calendar
flip as though they are caught in some covert draught.
These days I haven't time for people on television or
    aeroplanes
who say 'momentarily' meaning 'in just one moment'.

These days – these days which are fairly unremarkable –
light falls, outside of my window, on the red brick planes
where the trees are coming into leaf. These are the days
of correcting the grammar on library-desk graffiti,
the cheap, unmistakeable thrill of breaking a copyright
    law.

But these days, like Cleopatra's Antony, I fancy bestriding
    the ocean;
these days I am serious. These days I'm bowled over
hearing myself say *ten years ago this . . . ten years ago
    such-and-such*
like the man left standing, his house falling wall by wall,
in that black-and-white flick blurring headlong into
    colour.